Horatio Morpurgo's essays have appeared in *The London Magazine, The Edinburgh Review, Le Monde Diplomatique, New Internationalist, Areté* etc. and at *Three Monkeys Online. How Thomas Hardy Expressed His Doubt* was published in 2009, also by Erewhon Books. He studied at the Universities of Cambridge and Edinburgh and now lives in the South West of England.

DRAKE'S GRAFFITI

Coming Home Slowly to What the Sea Means

By
HORATIO MORPURGO

EREWHON BOOKS

Published by Erewhon Books
erewhonbooks@yahoo.co.uk

Printed in England by imprint*digital*.net

I.M. HW

The sea speaks a language polite people never repeat.
It is a colossal scavenger slang and has no respect.

Carl Sandberg, American poet, 1940

If you yourself can withstand three cheers at beholding these vivacious fish, then heaven help ye; the spirit of godly gamesomeness is not in ye.

Herman Melville on dolphins, 1851

…Navigation arithmetical… giveth longitudes and latitudes to the minute, second, and third… it teacheth the nature of angles and triangles… the quantities and proportions of parallels, the nature of Horizons… in Navigation… there can nothing be required, that by this heavenly harmony of numbers shall not be most copiously manifested to the Seamans admiration & great content.

John Davis, English sea captain, 1585

Preface

Only the tower and charred walls of St Andrew's were left standing in 1941, but that much of the building's medieval fabric could be, and was, scrubbed up and saved. During post-war restoration on one of the south-facing windows, a curious diagram was found carved into the sill. On a roughly drawn globe, the Equator and the two Tropics are energetically scored, criss-crossed with lines of longitude. From between the Equator and the Tropic of Cancer there emerge words in some jumbled and totally illegible script. Below and to the right sits the figure of a ship, sail hoisted and topmast pennon streaming: from its prow extends a rope that swerves up and around the world, as if it has only just been thrown. An enigmatic smaller boat floats free from the rest of the design, as if drawn to a different scale.

Known as 'the Drake Graffiti', a resemblance to certain elements in the great sea captain's coat of arms was quickly noticed. Otherwise the half-century and more since its discovery has added little to our understanding of it. The guidebooks all summarise it more or less thus: the local boy made good was home from sailing his ship around the world, the first Englishman ever to do so. In the ensuing Drake-mania this was a workman's doodle, done with the point of his trowel perhaps, before the plaster went on.

'It's crumbling away, I'm afraid.'

An elderly church warden had soundlessly approached. He was standing at my shoulder.

'Can you see it properly?' he inquired, anxious on my behalf.

'Fine, thank you.'

'You can't see it well enough because of all the light that comes through that window.' OK. He needs to talk. 'We tried filling it with tyre chalk – you know, that waxy stuff they mark the tyres with in your garage – we thought that would make it more visible, but that has started fading now as well.'

'It seems fine to me – maybe the tyre chalk treatment worked after all,' I compromised.

Apparently satisfied, he handed me a leaflet guide to the building then let me alone again.

It was the first time I'd seen the Drake Graffiti, which is strange enough in itself given that I grew up in the South West and even went to school for a while just down the road from here. But both the crude sketch in itself, belatedly discovered, and my reaction to it puzzled me. The indecipherable unruly script and the way that hawser hangs over the earth, half looping round it, still feel so eloquent, four centuries on, but eloquent of *what*?

Only now beginning to appreciate his story I saw how silly I'd been to resent that warden's 'intrusion'. I realised now, too late, that the tyre chalk was perfect. No museum curator, or only a very trendy one indeed, would ever have permitted such a 'conservation measure'. It was the secular equivalent of those tears they're forever 'refreshing' on Madonnas in Catholic countries. It's the curious rather than the credulous that St Andrew's Plymouth is putting out for but in these post-modern days is that distinction so clear? The tyre chalk was just right because it suggested that there is still something about Drake which the tourist information offices and the museums and the TV historians haven't quite got their hands on.

But why should any of this matter to me? I smiled and nodded at the warden on my way out and all seemed forgiven but there was something else in this, something further back, which explained why I was here writing this book about the sea at all. A piece of sixteenth century street art, never intended to be seen for more than a lunch break perhaps - dashed off in a few minutes as friends stood around – remains inscrutable the way dreams or certain childhood memories do. It shares their power through its origin in a never fully retrievable context, through an un-self-consciousness which our waking hours, like our adulthood, struggle to recover.

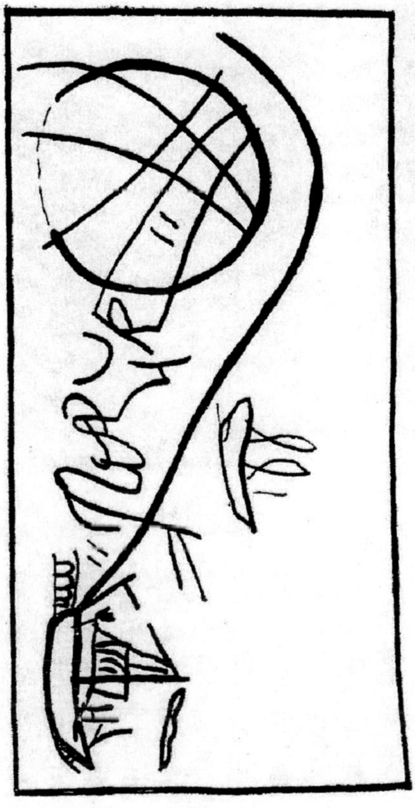

Figure 1 The Drake Graffiti, reproduced with the kind permission of the Rector of St Andrew's

Figure 2 Pink sea fan growing on a Lyme Bay scallop. John Worswick, who dives for scallops out of West Bay, took this photograph with his mobile telephone.

one

The letter's essential contents were two cloth badges which rolled into the palm of my hand as I opened it. The accompanying text could only say one thing but I read it where I stood anyway, aged eleven, in our icy hallway towards the end of the Christmas break. The badges: about the size of communion wafers, each with a white anchor on a black background. The cold: a blizzard on its way, thank God, about to block every possible exit out of here. For several days it permitted me to cheerfully dodge what that letter had said. I photographed snow-drifts instead and in the resulting images they still seem to glow with something of the gratitude I felt towards them. School was on the far side of the moor and the moor for now was impassable.

But a friend of my parents worked for the Forestry Commission and had access to a land rover. So I climbed at last into its freezing cab in greeny-grey shorts and watched my knees turn white as we rattled manfully along the treacherous lanes. On arrival the anchors sewn onto my jersey made me a prefect at a school where I'd been a new boy only the previous term. I saw clearly enough how well that would go down with the set of friends I had made so recently.

The dormitory of which I now had charge was called 'Hawkins'. The dormitories at this latest school were all named after naval heroes. Plymouth was close-by: my new insignia and the shoulder patches on our navy blue jerseys were intentionally martial-looking. Our sports teams were feared and the school took its maritime connections seriously. My parents had apparently opted for a bracing conservatism this time around. Their combined uncertainty about where to live, about how - and how far away - they wanted their own kids educated had this colourful if unintended consequence. Between the ages of eight and thirteen I attended a total of five different state primaries and boarding schools. My meteoric rise to prefect-hood, in other words, was unsettling perhaps but changing schools that often can be a school in itself. By now I thought of this varied diet as quite normal.

Neither was the naval atmosphere so very strange for Devon in the late Seventies. There was a Cold War on as well as a bad winter: many, even most of the boys were being paid for by the Ministry of Defence. NATO and the Warsaw Pact played war games in the North Atlantic,

Devonport prospered accordingly and we dressed the part. Somebody's father came to teach us about the Russian Navy, how to tell a Victor Class submarine from an Alpha Class one, a Kirov from a Moskva Class cruiser. Another father landed his green helicopter on a games field one afternoon to take some of us for an outing. Dartmoor as we over-flew it was rock-strewn and sheep-flecked. We circled above the prison and I remember I joked later that I'd sell the photographs I'd taken to the inmates one day. Witty little fellow. Adaptable, too.

But I come to the point about that figure scratched into the window-ledge. Francis Drake was born in the town which this school overlooked – there was a dormitory named after him as others were named after Raleigh and Grenville. Drake's Prayer was read at Remembrance Day services. As the sons of well-to-do local families it was expected I suppose that we identify with the Age of Discovery, or with the disproportionate role played in it by ships based in the West Country. To one suggestible eleven year-old the offer of being inscribed in such a pedigree was attractive. The link between this kind of education and the Tudorbethan villa in Surrey with a Jag out front is clear enough, but I would have had no idea what you were talking about, of course, if you had pointed it out to me then.

Were there / are there still, even, schools like this outside Seville and Lisbon, outside Le Havre or Amsterdam? I still have the book about Drake's circumnavigation, a good one, handed out as the prize in a poetry-reading competition. It must have been published as part of the 400th anniversary celebrations. The inscription says 'March 1979'. I see I complained bitterly to my diary about how foolish I'd been to get myself selected as a prefect and maybe I really did see it like that, but it was of course much more than the anchor on those badges that had got its hooks into me. Indomitably captained little craft making history in mid-ocean – I still think there are worse things to feed a child's imagination.

The Tudors had been a hobby for some time thanks to an excellent history teacher at a previous school – a peripatetic education, as I say, is not necessarily a bad one. So I was ready-primed for all this Drakery and Hawkinsism. More than 'primed' actually. We were taken to Buckland Abbey one summer afternoon – the house outside Plymouth, that is, which Drake bought (from Grenville) on his treasure-laden return. I see from what I wrote in the same diary that evening that my hero had calmly walked into the Great Hall as I lingered to admire the portraits: 'I had an amazing feeling… Francis Drake walked in. I could imagine everything'.

It's a pretty bare mention, considering. You'd think I might have recorded some part of what he said at least. I remember the atmosphere and the portraits in that hall very clearly but I'd forgotten, until I came across that entry recently, that he'd put in a personal appearance. We'll come back to this incident but sketchily described encounters with long deceased persons might seem more affecting than they do if so much of this had not been underwritten by the military establishment. And there is one very powerful memory I have which suggests some awareness of this.

One of the teachers, HW, owned a small yacht which he had acquired in northern Germany at the end of the Second World War. This was a Drakean act which I admired – or quite possibly invented, now that I think about it, accomplished young fantasist that I was. Anyway the oddest thing about HW to me then, though I find it less odd now, was that he had a rotten temper and wasn't much of a teacher. But as soon as we were out of the school gates he knew exactly where to go and what to do. He knew a lot about architecture and was a birdwatcher and I am surely not alone in having been led by him to examine the world much more closely than I otherwise might have.

He would drive a few of us down to where his boat was moored, some miles above Plymouth on the River Tamar. Together we explored the thickly wooded labyrinth of waterways and tidal creeks that reach into the countryside behind the city. It's a 'drowned valley system' in the geographer's parlance, submerged at the end of the last ice age. Or when I later came across that 'nook-shotten isle' phrase in *Henry V* it was immediately those outings I thought of.

I've been on the look-out ever since, in a way, for a better understanding of what those water-born weekends were about. There are some experiences which turn into memory by a process of accumulation – they are sedimentary or metamorphic rather than igneous memories. Those long afternoons, with tidal waters obeying their own slow laws around us, were my earliest intimation of this perhaps.

Other memories by contrast establish themselves as quick as a flash, like the one I mean to relate here. We sailed right down into Plymouth Sound one grey September afternoon then out beyond the breakwater. The aircraft-carrier *Ark Royal* was moored off Devonport at that time - the Navy's flagship for twenty years, it had just been de-commissioned. We'd seen it on the news – about how it was laid down in the 1940s and took ten years to build. It would shortly be removed to a scrap-yard and there were no plans to replace it with a ship of similar size.

Piecing together the rest wasn't so hard. It had been built to meet the needs of an Empire which no longer existed. Several of the teachers at that school, HW among them, had worked in Kenya before independence and Rhodesia had become Zimbabwe just a year or two previously. The new *Ark Royal* would be much smaller, better suited to the country's reduced circumstances. Also better suited to chasing Russian submarines around the North Atlantic which was, as we knew better than most children our age, what the Navy now did.

We approached this mighty emblem of The End as close as a line of buoys allowed. The binoculars we had brought along for golden plover and herons were turned on this looming steel cliff, rusting all the way round where it met the water-line. So absorbed we must have been in contemplation of this gigantic guano-spattered gull-roost that we gave a collective jump when our keel struck something. It was like being tapped on the shoulder when you think you're alone. Flagships and the Past Imperial were forgotten in a moment. There was a watery scuffling somewhere close-by and suddenly a cormorant was paddling about right next to the boat with a large fish wriggling furiously in its beak.

The bird, it was immediately apparent, had been surfacing in a hurry and in mid-struggle with its prey. It seemed like us now to be taking in several things at once – the unexpected size and strength of its catch, the obstacle against which it had just cracked its head through not looking out, and that row of humans, mainly juvenile, staring as usual, perched along the rim of - whatever those damn things they float about in are called.

On all of which it had no time to waste if it wanted to keep this fish. The bird and its dignity between them quickly worked out a solution, which was to commence beating large black wings, to plough a messy line as straight as they could make it, directly away from us. Sliding to a halt some way off, it found sufficient privacy to concentrate. Down went the fish in three or four uncomfortable-looking gulps. Only then did it glance complacently back at that half a dozen pairs of raised binoculars. Or perhaps it was really just eying up a former flagship as somewhere to hang its wings out to dry while a large and still lively meal was digesting.

*

The rock in Plymouth Sound which we passed a little later, encrusted now with four centuries' worth of fortifications, was pointed out to us as 'Drake's Island'. HW told exactly the same story as I'd found in that book. Again, I find that less odd now than I did then. It was off this island that Drake weighed anchor in September 1580, thereby completing his circumnavigation of the globe. Famously he hesitated here before entering Sutton Harbour proper. His last landfall had been Sierra Leone, his state of knowledge about England was three years out of date and these were wildly unsteady times. Approaching Plymouth he hailed a passing boat: 'Is the Queen still living?' is said to have been the first question he asked.

I wonder now whether there might not have been some other reason to hesitate on the very point of 'return' – was it really just that they were such canny sea-dogs? The politics of what they were returning to may well have seemed at least as daunting as those ocean currents they had just ridden round the world. But might this not also have been the moment when the full scale of their achievement hit home? Here they took their leave of it, in one sense, before it passed out of their hands to take on all the meanings it would have now for others.

As the *Golden Hind* stood warily off-shore that November afternoon, the Mayor of Plymouth and Drake's wife set out on board another ship to reassure him. 'Drake's Island', until then, had been 'St Nicholas' Island' – St Nicholas revered as the patron saint of sailors. In Protestant England they had a new one now. His reputation of course has risen, has fallen, has shape-shifted down the centuries and continues to do so. But that habits of veneration could be re-directed in this way, such that local schoolboys four centuries later are still picking up residual traces of the cult, is surely passing strange.

As with that Graffiti, the story and its scenery have a power over me which I can't fully explain. There's so much about it that we still don't know. Unfamiliar with the coast of Brazil, Drake 'employed' the services of a Portuguese pilot whom he had captured earlier off the Cape Verde Islands. Later released, this pilot gave an account of Drake which has survived and is not unfavourable. 'He carries a book in which he writes his log and paints birds, trees and seals. He is diligent in painting…'[1] Apparently there was a boy on board who knew how to draw and acted as his assistant. Drake is said to have delivered that logbook to the Queen by hand on his return. It has never been seen since. How is such a book 'lost' and why? What were the paintings like? Who was the boy and what happened to him?

HW would take us to the Isles of Scilly in the holidays: spring migrants arrive there, and the milder weather with them, before either arrive anywhere else. The archipelago which forms the south-westernmost bit of English territory was originally one of a sequence of mountain ranges – on the mainland Bodmin Moor and Dartmoor are its much-eroded continuations. North American strays not infrequently make their first exhausted landfall there, but the islands lie similarly in the path of birds travelling north or south. All of which lends the place an atmosphere of sanctuary. It's that atmosphere, I'd guess, which most visitors are really in search of, whether they bring telescopes on tripods or not.

Sandy lagoons stretch their aquamarine transparencies between the islands. They say at low tide you can wade across between some of them, but I never have. Connected to the mainland by ferry and to the world by ocean currents and the flight-paths of migratory birds, the islands lie low in the water, wide open to the four cardinal points. I think to myself now how that man must have hated his week-day / term-time persona that he was such an ingenious escape artist from it. School-life and home-life were, the both of them, over there somewhere, well below the eastern horizon. Here and for now were sandwich terns arriving from West Africa. In the cobbled streets of Hugh Town, turnstones checked for sand-hoppers under every scrap of rubbish or seaweed. They fluttered round your feet, quite untroubled by human beings from having hatched out on the Arctic tundra. Books about Drake might cover similar distances in a way but here it felt as if we were staring straight into them, as if these birds were their messengers.

We kept getting lucky with the weather – that must be why I remember everything so blue and white. Was it fine weather, then, or a teacher generous with his holidays, or just being twelve? Or maybe it was the Space Program. On our final visit we were allowed one afternoon to sit in the bar of the Atlantic Hotel and watch the first launching of the Space Shuttle *Columbia.*

Our run of luck with the weather had finally broken - a bank of thick fog had rolled in earlier that day. We'd stumbled pointlessly about in it listening to the St Mary's fog horn all morning: the weird outdoor claustrophobia made it all the more reassuring to have four walls around us again. And how to express the mystery of being allowed in a bar at twelve or thirteen, the enigma of drink, the smell of beer-mats? Adulthood was more jealous of its privileges then. The clear skies of Florida vicariously enjoyed, history in the making and ordering drinks were, between them, consolation enough for any change in the weather.

Off *Columbia* went, slowly at first, until the blue around it deepened and the camera was less steady at the higher and higher magnifications required. The orbiter and its booster went grainy and dim, hardly visible above that fireball, so when a change came over them you couldn't immediately tell what had happened. But it must have been that the solid fuel rocket had disengaged because now you saw it, separate and slowing, falling back towards the Atlantic below as the manned craft continued on its way.

Once the first sailing into Plymouth Sound or the first visit to the Scilly Isles has happened, once the Space Shuttle has blasted off in the bar of the Atlantic Hotel and the book about Drake has been read, these together establish themselves as a kind of symbolic shorthand. Our later selves refer back - to what it all meant then - or forwards, to the more or less or to the something quite different which it comes to mean later, in the light of fresh understanding. Out of that unique and private language, or out of the resulting conversation, rather, between past and present selves which we carry on in it, there emerges the person we come to be.

I think this is something like what psychologists call 'individuation'. It's a delicate process to begin with. How much of what we

term 'parenting' or 'schooling' really assists in it? There's no objective measure but if either has been done well, that tends to mean the process has been discreetly assisted. HW and the sea, for example, assisted. Parenting or schooling can be said to have been done badly in so far as this process has either been neglected or actively disrupted. Something with the sea around it which comprised the Elizabethans and the South West generally, and the Scillies and bird-watching in particular, established itself with me, very early, as a 'language' of this kind.

Years after HW and my time at that school, about to depart for university, I took down the book about Drake's circumnavigation again. I'd started to travel myself by this time and had also got back to reading what I felt like after the interruption of A-levels. It was a much-changed England to which Drake returned in 1580, a changed man himself. On the eve of my own departure I took down that book again.

two

Faking up personal encounters with its subject was no longer necessary. Paradoxically, though, I'd have had a better idea what to ask him by now and I'd have taken much more care to record his answers, too. I'd viewed the moor mainly from my bedroom window and from the countryside around my home but I knew that it was visible, on the far side, from well out at sea: what, if anything, did the sight of it mean to Drake, I wondered?

Folktales about Drake flourished in the West Country even during his own life-time, as he must have been aware. What did he make of them? He was widely thought of as an enchanter: his having 'shot the gulf' (i.e. his having made it into the Pacific) was proof of magical powers. As Mayor of Plymouth he would later bring clean water into the city off the moor by constructing a leat. This too morphed into stories about how the water had followed magically at his horse's heels as he rode into town one morning.

Such stories probably express, as well as admiration, the widespread uneasiness to which the new mathematical sciences gave rise - navigation and engineering included. But I'd discovered anthropology by now and there are non-western cultures in which long-distance travel is also an activity with magical associations – not least in the very Pacific region Drake was returning from. The Trobriand Islands, Hawaii and Eastern Papua New Guinea have all furnished anthropologists with examples.[2] How would he have responded to hearing about that? Drake as a young man had taken part in two slaving expeditions – a subject my old book about the circumnavigation had ignored. I'd have been wanting some answers to that as well by now.

But above all this: on his return he incorporated the two pole stars, north and south, into his coat of arms. He had captained the ship which gave the English their first glimpse of just how wide and new the world now was. Shakespeare would have been sixteen when he heard the news and could hardly have been indifferent to it. Or if it turned out Sir Francis wasn't much of a theatre-goer, if he failed to be impressed or even flattered by this reference, I might save face by quoting very briefly from an exact contemporary, and a seaman like himself: *Within these last 80 yeares, that have so much enlarged the boundes of the Worlde, that nowe we have twice or thrice so much scope for our earthlie peregrinations, as we have had in times past…*[3] How did such sentiments weigh with him, as against the loot he brought back, say? Was he aware of how his voyage had changed the way the world now felt for the people he was returning to?

We say lazily of Renaissance England – and we do the same with certain episodes in our own personal development - that categories of thought and feeling were being overthrown as others were set up in their place. But how much sense do such formulations ever make *at the time*? Drake might be employing the very latest in navigational science but during the Atlantic crossing he accused one of his crew of being a witch and would later execute him on the coast of what is now Argentina. Indeed their quarrel began as the boat's supplies were being loaded, even before they left Plymouth. Drake's having passed from one plane of the earth's surface to another, as we've seen, struck many of his contemporaries as the act of a sorcerer. A bombed-out mediaeval church, Drake's graffiti, tyre chalk: we might be surprised at how familiar to him this volatile mixture of the modern with the pre-modern would have seemed.

*

Second-year students each received forty pounds from the college to spend on any books they liked. It was intended to encourage us to explore. I hope those forty pounds still happen, adjusted for inflation. One of the books I bought was a biography of John Dee. It wasn't a book I needed directly for any of the courses I was taking. It was unfinished Elizabethan business you might say: the memory of that giant gull-roost parked in the entrance to the River Tamar was already prompting a new kind of question - things move quickly at that age.

My questioning by now was less about Drake and his particular exploits, more about the nature of the impulse *behind* all this exploration. I'd begun at the same time to work out what I wanted from university – I had some discovering to do, too. Marginally less 'adaptable' these days I read a lot, not much of it anything to do with my courses. I chased a pretty girl and when she broke my heart I joined the Astronomy Society. I wrote odd articles for the student paper and was just then capping it all by directing my very own and mainly dreadful production of *Anthony and Cleopatra.*

I remember my surprise at learning that while he was where I was now John Dee had got interested in the theatre. The job he'd been given was teaching Greek, in 1547, the first year after the college was founded. He soon departed for continental universities where the new mathematics – his real interest at this stage - was held in higher esteem. Still, he found the time to invent a mechanical device which was used during a production of *Peace* by Aristophanes, put on in the dining hall. It seems to have worked fine. Even a little too fine. There was speculation that the young 'Doctor Dee' must be 'smutted with the black art', i.e. that he was practising witchcraft.

No murmurings of witchcraft greeted my own theatrical efforts. The best that can be said of them was that they did expose, as planned, one shaggy-haired history student to the language of *Anthony and Cleopatra* for a month or so. But I rejoiced to discover that I had, if nothing else, then some of these buildings around me, at least, in common with John Dee. He is at any age one of the best because one of the most puzzling ways into the English Renaissance. Court intriguer and cutting-edge mathematician, navigator and mystic, Greek scholar and champion of all things Welsh, legal and metallurgical advisor to the government, all-purpose political consultant, necromancer, tutor to Philip Sidney and Robert Dudley, astrologer to the Queen.

For our purposes here he was above all ardent in the cause of what he himself called 'this British discovery and recovery enterprise.' It has more recently been termed 'the Cathay Campaign': the search for a 'Northwest Passage', a shipping route to China round the top of North America and access thereby to Far Eastern markets. English settlement in the New World was initially planned as a series of trading-posts along that route.

Dee was close to the circle which backed Drake's voyage and it seems more than likely that Drake's long detour up the coast of California in 1578 was a search for the western end of this non-existent strait. Dee's advice was being sought around the same time by many other explorers and pilots. But according to him the purpose of all this discovery was not only new markets, it was also 'to penetrate the secrets of the universe'[4]. Writing his *Famous and Rich Discoveries* in mid-1577, at a time when Drake's expedition was the only one being prepared, Dee described the voyages of discovery to the Queen: 'Of how great importance then to you is that attempt which is by a British Subject presently intended to God's glory, the benefit of all Christendom, and the honour and profit of this realm chiefly,' as well as 'to the contentment of many a noble mind which delighteth to understand how *the earth is the Lord's and the fullness thereof...*' The journeys were justified by a universal 'law of Nature', which offered to man 'the whole Ball & Sphericall frame of the erth & water'. In return this 'law' required only that man 'be to the O*mn*ipotent Creator, sincerely thankfull & to the humayn society, friendly & comfortable.'[5] To view the sending out of these ships as an exclusively and aggressively political and commercial affair, then, or likewise to dismiss the other motives involved as mere window-dressing, does not actually fit all the evidence.

For more than three centuries after his death in obscurity, Dee was neglected in histories of the period and this was doubtless a function of his many contradictions. But which would startle an educated Elizabethan more, I wonder: that John Dee was ignored for three centuries, or the interest he has attracted more recently? The change came only in 1930, with Eva Taylor's account of Dee as navigator in her *Tudor Geography*.

Navigation was crucial to Dee's vision of how the new science could transform his country's prospects. A great and lifelong teacher, the lectures on Euclid which he gave in Paris after leaving Cambridge caused such a stir that he was invited to remain as Royal Mathematician to the court of Henri III. He declined the offer and returned instead to England, bringing various globes and compasses with him. He was soon writing the preface to the first ever translation of Euclid into English. Writing 'to stirre the imagination mathematicall: and to inform ye practise mechanicall,' he argued there for the urgent need to apply this revival of Greek geometry in all aspects of his country's economic life. He regarded navigation as crucial to this, a skill in which English seamen at this time lagged far behind their Iberian and Italian counterparts.

In the longer term the suspicions he had met with at Cambridge were never quite allayed. Accusations of sorcery dogged his career and finally ruined his reputation. But his reinstatement, when it finally came, was taken up by Frances Yates and several of her students: by the early 1960s Dee had been restored to his place at the very centre of the English Renaissance project. He has since grown into a medium-sized academic industry, with a major conference in 2006 and another in 2009 to mark the four hundredth anniversary of his death.

If he has for the better part of a century now held his place at the centre of that project, his reputation remains as fiercely contested as ever. You could even be forgiven for asking whether the controversy has taken on a meaning of its own, semi-independent of its subject. To some he remains what his detractors maintained all along – a scientist of no great distinction and a courtier of no lasting significance, whose turn to the occult was a measure of his disappointment with life. He was a peripheral not to say delusional figure, taken up or dropped by the powerful as their interests dictated.

For others the range of his skills inspires awe – he was the magus figure at the heart of the changes his culture underwent on this brink of modernity. His pupils and close associates would variously lead expeditions to what we now call the Canadian Arctic, start the fashion for writing sonnets, introduce the ideas of Copernicus to an English audience, act as scientific adviser to, then chronicler of, the first English settlement in the New World.

But whatever view we take of this perplexing figure in his Elizabethan context, there is one less avoidable question which he raises: what was it about the mid-twentieth century that suddenly made his career a matter of such urgent concern to scholars and artists alike? There is a clue perhaps in a phrase from that *Preface to Euclid*, that by navigation 'might grow Commoditye, to this land chiefly, and to the rest of the Christen Common wealth, farre passing all riches and earthly Threasure.'

'Commodity far passing all riches and earthly treasure'. Whatever Drake was personally in it for, it seems that the 'Cathay Campaign', for some of its backers and for Dee, might well fill England's coffers, but its true value was a less obvious one. Dee's travels on the Continent would have brought him face to face with an atmosphere of bitter religious acrimony. A sense of catastrophic breach with the past colours the whole of this Reformation period in Europe and for someone raised Catholic, as Dee was, in what was now a Protestant country, this sense of impending apocalypse would have been keenly felt.

It seems likely that he cast Elizabeth in a semi-messianic role, as the figure who by taking on a global role could both reform and redeem this situation, always assuming she kept Dee on as her advisor. At the same time alchemical traditions of Arabic origin, which Dee and many of his contemporaries took seriously, had long suggested that the Philosopher's Stone was to be sought in China. Eclectic as ever, Dee combined his own patriotic search for it with the latest scientific advances, and both of these with the need for access to China's fabled wealth in particular and that of the Far East more generally.

This was the route by which he arrived at an imperial programme for England which was at once a political and economic, as well as an intellectual or spiritual enterprise. From the late 1560s to the mid 1580s Dee was a crucial figure at Elizabeth's court. His advice was in demand and he wrote widely, both for publication and for private circulation, on what England's new maritime Empire would mean and how it necessitated a permanent Navy. He died poor and ridiculous but in one form or another much of what he advised came to pass, even if so much of what he intended by his advice was missed.

And this is why Dee came to matter again in the twentieth century. What we now call the 'scientific revolution' did not arrive fully formed. The term itself is of recent origin – it was first used in its modern meaning, significantly enough, in 1943[6], by Alexandre Moyré. The origins of that 'revolution' are, in fact, rather too contradictory for comfort and nobody embodies those contradictions more fully than Dee. Mid-twentieth century Europe watched its empires melting away, surveyed its own burnt-out cities and decimated populations and found it no longer possible to think of science as the 'disinterested' adventure it had long presented itself as being. Its advances, it was now clear, threatened the very world they had been devised to explain. There was naturally much reflection upon what had gone wrong.

Dee had urged his country to exploit the revived Greek learning and the technical advances associated with it. But for him this had been part of a deeply moral project. Modern Europeans needed now as a matter of urgency to understand what the collapse of confidence in their project meant, whether in fact any of that confidence could survive its disastrous misapplications. Dee's career suddenly seemed a good place to start digging.

That career was both inseparable from and every bit as varied as his social network: he conducted, for example, a passionate campaign to rescue the libraries of English monasteries as they were plundered through the 1540s and 1550s. Samuel Taylor Coleridge would argue in 1830 that the monasteries should have been turned into cultural and educational centres[7], rather than simply sold to the new plutocrats (as with Drake's own Buckland Abbey).

Coleridge may have been a towering Romantic genius but he was also several centuries late. Dee was not only thinking like this as the situation unfolded around him, he also put himself at personal risk and acted on his convictions. Through his salvage work, and from his many continental journeys, he built up the largest book collection anywhere in England at the time, and one which he kept in Mortlake as a *hospitali philosophorum peregrinatum*, a 'hostelry for wandering philosophers'. This amounted to a kind of independent research institute and it was here that he instructed pilots in the new navigational science.

At the moment of Europe's highest religious tensions, then, he kept open house for the best minds of his day. He cultivated personal friendships with the best English scientists, Francis Bacon among them, as with Portugal's Cosmographer Royal and the Dutch cartographer Mercator, Hungarian mining engineers, an Italian Benedictine spiritual advisor, Polish princes and Bohemian noblemen. His insistence upon this cosmopolitanism even as Europe slid towards religious civil war is surely one of the bravest and most appealing things about him. Knowledge of every kind was the 'commodity' which he hoped might save Europe from itself by bringing about a renewed awareness of what connects us to each other, to the wider world and to the universe beyond.

three

Re-decorating upstairs I could look out now over roof-tops and through a mesh of telephone wires at a bit of blue infill on my horizon. This was what the estate agent had coyly advertised as a 'sea glimpse'. My new neighbours told me about the days in winter when you can hear waves thumping into the coastal defences two miles away and I heard it myself soon enough. I told myself walking over the fields to a beach beat walking down a street to the Thames at any time of the year. I fished a bit and went snorkelling, or read up about the fossils which fall out of the cliffs here, but these all felt like stock responses in some way I couldn't quite put my finger on.

As a new recruit to bird-watching, I'd joined my local Wildlife Trust at the age of twelve and through some combination of laziness and loyalty never cancelled my membership. The magazine it went on sending me landed on my door-mat one morning twenty-five years later and I learnt of its campaign for a ban on scallop-dredging in Lyme Bay, where that walk across the fields now took me. I went on travelling a lot for magazine assignments after I first moved back to the West Country and the move made relatively little difference to that at first. The move had felt like a natural progression in some way I didn't need to explain and my not needing to explain it was what made the impulse feel trustworthy.

I do need to explain this though: scallop-dredgers drag rows of large steel spikes across the sea-bed and the damage they do has been exhaustively documented. The damage being done to sponges, pink sea fans and cold water corals got completely out of hand in Lyme Bay when the price of diesel started rising: more boats than ever were attracted to a fishery which cost little to reach. There was also no quota on scallops and the TV chefs loved them. I was already looking for a way to involve myself in this campaign when a large freighter in the Channel obliged me by starting to break up during a January gale. Deliberately run aground in Lyme Bay, so that it could be salvaged, about a hundred of the containers stacked on its deck were lost overboard. A few of them washed up on a nearby beach and were looted.

The campaign of a local Wildlife Trust to stop scallop-dredging is not news, as several editors had already pointed out to me, but an oil-spill was and so was this horde of latter-day wreckers. So in the guise of writing about the one

I got to write about the other, and interviewed several people in my area I'd wanted to meet for a while now – fishermen, biologists, activists. It felt perverse to view this occasion as a stroke of good luck, but such is the logic of the current affairs industry. I'd claimed to be looking for a way to write that didn't mean jumping in aeroplanes quite so regularly – well… this oil-spill might be read as a grimly ironical message addressed precisely to people who make such claims, couldn't it?

The MS *Napoli* leaked its fuel-oil and scattered its cargo and I had written my article, when, in an unrelated development, Her Majesty's Government decided that my wife must now, as a foreign resident, pass a 'Citizenship Test'. This test is more expensive than true-born English might imagine, but no doubt the inconvenience is all part of its appeal for HM Gov. As the date we'd been given approached my wife duly mugged up on how many MPs can dance on the head of a pin, then I dropped her off at some council offices on the edge of Plymouth. Plymouth had turned out to be the closest test-centre for us.

Rather than waiting there I drove into town, parked in the Drake Centre and idled the time away escorting our toddler up and down the moving stairways and elevators of that many-storied and gleaming retail development. We went for a saunter outside and the time passed soon enough. She'd already had the result by the time we arrived (her score was 100%) so we just drove home, relieved and amused.

But something had occurred to me in the Drake Centre, then again in the shopping streets behind it. I had been to school no distance from here but felt scarcely any more connection with this town in itself than my wife did. I 'knew' what I did know about it in such a way that I hardly knew *it* at all.

It must have been from HW's yacht, so from the river that afternoon, that I first saw Plymouth. I'd passed through the railway station a few times since. But who, now, I asked myself, apart from people on yachts and people on holiday, sees Plymouth for the first time from the water? Only one autumn morning, having just turned forty, did it strike me just how baffling that school's attitude to its nearest city was. I see from my diaries that we played no sports against Plymouth schools and went on no trips there. It wasn't, as I've indicated, that we ignored it exactly, but how *archaic* the way we framed it!

I suppose in some sense education is always a form of conscription – in the case of that particular school perhaps more literally than most. But such an omission seems so unaccountable - as if it formed part of a curriculum so unofficial it didn't even need to be taught as such. In their end of term reports I remember the teachers forever lamenting the 'many gaps' in my knowledge – i.e. lamenting that my parents had not started purchasing their educational product sooner. But look now at this gap in what they taught us – a gap the size of modern Plymouth, one of the West Country's less affluent cities.

So helicopter-rides and blissful bird-watching trips aside, was that an 'education' or was it poison bait? I was reminded now of the Great Transistor Radio Scare. Some boys were discovered to be in possession of transistor radios and there was a panic about covert listening to the Top Forty. I still can't hear some tunes on the radio without being reminded of how this anodyne pap was once dignified with forbidden status. There's no reason why children shouldn't be made fully aware of the alternatives to chart music, but was that crack-down on transistors really about music? Or was it rather of a piece with those other omissions, like that of a certain city nearby, which went to make up our unofficial curriculum?

One great reason for studying the thought of the past, and of other cultures, is that it gives us a perspective from which we can actually see and criticise the ideas we have grown up with.[8]

A Marine Protected Area (MPA) in Lyme Bay was announced the following year, in July 2008. I was there when the Minister announced it, having drafted responses to consultations and written stroppy letters for a local environmental group. After the initial euphoria my first response was to ask a philosopher to come and give a talk, taking this development as the starting-point for some more general reflections. The philosopher I had in mind once translated a superb essay by a Czech writer on a comparable theme, but he didn't want to do it and I let the idea lapse. Other minds must have been running along similar lines, however: the local Wildlife Trust was suddenly in touch asking if I wanted to give a lecture on it, something about 'what the sea means', perhaps.

I agreed. And then I worried. Ask a question as wide open as what the sea means and it's really another kind of question you're asking first. Given that the sea means so many different things to so many people, what kind of 'meaning' has priority over which other kind? Which forms of knowledge matter most? Why? It's the kind of question, in other words, to which the answer we give is likely to be self-revealing.

The Lyme Bay MPA was the outcome of a particular and long-running dispute, mainly between the Wildlife Trusts and a lobbying group set up by the scallop-dredgers to obstruct any change in the law. But once that particular argument had been settled, the resulting reserve, as the first of any size in English waters, and the recovery of its sea-bed, took on a wider symbolic importance (figure 2). This *was* the right occasion to ask a more general question about what the sea had meant or might now start meaning to us. I'd already thought as much myself. But how to *say* that?

Having no idea where to begin, for several months I asked friends, acquaintances and perfect strangers. A tourist said it meant the opposite of her office and a teenager was able to confirm that the sea means freedom. A fisherman said it meant his livelihood. A writer described almost drowning in the Black Sea. A frequent traveller to the Middle East compared it to the desert.

Nothing of what they said went into the talk I gave, or not consciously, and none of the personal associations which I've described here. I wanted to be 'objective'. I've been less so now, although this text grew out of the talk I eventually gave. The West Country's relationship with the sea is a famously long and complicated one. The way it has marked and continues to mark individual lives is a legitimate line of inquiry, alongside all the others.

My research for the talk, becoming more serious as the date approached, took me in a new direction again, or, rather, in a very ancient one. Dee, as I've said, started out as a lecturer in Greek, mainly because that was the only language in which the mathematical texts he was really interested in could then be studied. I knew I'd say something about the Age of Discovery but it was time to go back now, beyond the Elizabethans, to understand better where they themselves had been coming from.

If one had to expound the doctrine of antiquity with utmost brevity while standing on one leg, as Hillel did that of the Jews, it could only be in this sentence: 'They alone shall possess the earth who live from the powers of the cosmos.' Nothing distinguishes the ancient from the modern man so much as the former's absorption in a cosmic experience scarcely known to later periods. Its waning is marked by the flowering of astronomy at the beginning of the modern age. Kepler, Copernicus, and Tycho Brahe were certainly not driven by scientific impulses alone. All the same, the exclusive emphasis on an optical connection to the universe, to which astronomy very quickly led, contained a portent of what was to come.[9]

Miletus in the seventh and sixth centuries BC was a maritime community situated on what is now the west coast of Turkey. Unusually enterprising, its overland trading with Babylon, and its trading by sea with Egypt, brought it into regular contact with civilisations much older than its own. They were also civilisations which had sophisticated if relatively static mathematical traditions, from which it is certain that the Milesians eagerly learnt.

They founded the trading station of Naucratis in the Nile Delta, as well as colonies right along the northern and western shores of the Black Sea and in southern Italy. Small wonder that one of the earliest 'world maps' in existence was made in the sixth century BC by one Hecetaeus of Miletus (see figure 4 – the City of Plymouth Museum has a copy of it on the wall). This cartographer was a historian too (the very first, according to Herodotus) but his own achievement was only part of a larger one, which is of the deepest significance for the later development of western science.

Because what also arose in this small but teeming centre was a group of thinkers known to the Greeks as φγσιϰοι – 'physikoi' - from φγσις – 'physis' – the Greek word for 'nature'. 'Physikoi' meant 'those who speculate about the natural world'. They engaged fully in the life of their city, including its foreign ventures - the very first of them, Thales, made a fortune trading in olive oil with Egypt, where he also appears to have studied. He correctly predicted a solar eclipse in May of 585 BC from which historians have dated the starting-point of their intellectual adventure.

They wrote books about navigation, geometry and astronomy and their lead was soon taken up in neighbouring Greek communities, on the island of Samos, for example, where the great mathematician Pythagoras was born. What was distinctive about the physikoi was that they attempted, for the first time, a purely naturalistic explanation of the natural world. Thales, for example, argued that all matter was really water under various degrees of compression or rarefaction: the conclusions they drew about nature seem strange to us but their method marks a new departure. They are honoured as the first self-consciously 'scientific' thinkers.

Their successors would give us the first atomic theory, developed by Democritus of Abdera, as well as the discovery of the optic nerve and of the brain as the main sensory centre, by Alcmaeon of Crotone. They were what eventually led to Aristotle dissecting sponges in his attempt to classify them and the beginnings of what we call natural history. Such materialism had its opponents even then but there were some among these proto-scientists who cannot be described as materialists quite: Pythagoras, for example, credited by the ancients as the inventor of music, was certainly a politician and a mystic as well as the mathematician and geometer we all learnt about at school. Number was 'the pattern in God's mind as He created', as Boethius[10] would put it a thousand years later, and as Dee would agree another thousand years after that. Already for Pythagoras number was the reality underlying the universe: properly understood, it fused the religious and the mathematical.

It was a follower of his, Aristarchus, also from Samos, who was the first to argue, in the third century BC, that it is the earth which revolves around the sun, not the other way round, and furthermore that it was only doing what all the other planets do as well. It was a view he expressed tentatively from fear of being charged with impiety[11] (as we've seen, that argument is a little older than certain best-selling polemicists would have us believe). It was knowledge and controversy, both, which the revival of Greek brought with it to sixteenth century Europe.

Copernicus' *De Revolutionibus* appeared in 1543, presenting new mathematical proofs confirming this ancient theory that it was the earth which revolved round the sun. Copernicus was quite explicit that his insight was not new and his ideas were first promoted in England, some time later (see figure 3) as fully in accordance with 'the most ancient doctrines of the Pythagoreans etc.' That is to say, in accordance with theories which had begun with the 'physikoi' of Miletus.

It was precisely the moment of this revival which Dee chose to study the new mathematics on the continent. He returned to England in 1551 with two globes, on which were represented the latest theories about the shape of the world's continents. He also brought back astronomical instruments made by Gemma Phrysius, the first man to publish a treatise on the method of surveying by triangulation.

It was Gemma's view, for example, as those globes will have shown – and as we've already discussed - that there existed a shipping route round the top of North America by which the Far East could be reached. Not to mince matters, he labelled the strait as follows *Per hoc fretum iter est ad Mollucas* – 'Through these straits lies the way to the Spice Islands.'

Dee was to invest personally in several journeys to find this Passage in the 1570s and 1580s. He wrote a treatise on navigation in 1576, the year before Drake left. In the emergence of Greek science, as during its re-discovery two thousand years later, the sea and the need to cross

Figure 3 Frontispiece from the first book in English to expound the ideas of Copernicus (1572). The sun is shown at the centre: note that this is described as a 'most ancient doctrine of the Pythagoreans, etc'.

Figure 4 A 'map of the world', by Hecetaeus of Miletus, sixth century BC

it safely were at the heart of developments in astronomy, geometry and cartography. Directly or indirectly, for good and for ill, it was from our relationship with the sea that science first emerged.

But surely this is obvious, you say. And how, in the age of television history, can I write as if there were no widespread awareness of these things? Environmentalists routinely urge us, and with some reason, to see our world a new way and yes, the Renaissance would be the most obvious historical parallel for the scale of the change that's needed. But trust our TV historians – they'll have known how to strike the right note.

I select three examples at random. In the Elizabethan episode of Simon Schama's *A History of Britain* neither Dee nor Drake is mentioned. The Armada, to illustrate, was not defeated in the Channel at all but by Elizabeth's speech at Tilbury. Where is the author of *Landscape and Memory* or *The Embarrassment of Riches* in this reduction of the English Renaissance to Tudor family drama? David Starkey, in his own account of Elizabeth's reign, is so sure he twice insists that the port Drake returned to from his circumnavigation was Southampton. A trifling slip of the pen. Starkey wears a business suit throughout: he mentions Dee as an astrologer and is also clear that the expedition's purpose was purely commercial and political. The hit series COAST, following a BBC reporter around the British shoreline, naturally took in Plymouth. Its presenter strolled along Sutton Quay with a younger, casually dressed historian who was able to reveal that Drake's wealth was all made in the slave trade.

On this new televisual reading, then, Drake makes his fortune out of the two slaving expeditions in which he participated during his twenties. It may sound like hair-splitting, but it's not clear to me how he can have made any money at all from these voyages. On the first they were tricked into landing a large part of their 'cargo' without payment. From the second Drake was lucky to escape with his life when the enterprise was ambushed by Spanish ships. He later made common cause with run-away slaves in Spanish America just as he did with Native Indians: not, of course, because he was any kind of multiculturalist, but because he was an astute strategist. Why search the sixteenth century for multiculturalism in our sense of the term just so you can be disappointed to 'learn' that it didn't exist?

Again, contrary to popular superstition Drake felt no attachment to his native county but moved to Southampton at the first opportunity and there began to lead a life of leisure on his ill-gotten gains. He went on business-trips now and again, some of them quite long ones, but far too much has been read into the 'circumnavigation', so-called.

He roused himself from this torpid routine to destroy the Spanish fleet in Cadiz one weekend - out of sheer spite - when the force being readied there meant his country no harm at all. Tiresomely repetitious, he then needlessly destroyed Spain's replacement fleet only a year later, as it was cruising innocently up the Channel. This last stunt is particularly hard to forgive since Elizabeth had already dressed up specially: she looked absolutely stunning as she stated categorically that the invasion would not succeed. So there was no need for any fighting at all, you see.

I caricature, but why this studious avoidance of the larger issues which were at stake here? Or, when they are faced, why the complacent generalisations, whether celebratory or damning?

I realise, before you say it, that it is to our credit that we don't sentimentalise Drake. The speed with which the other side of the Atlantic, once reached, was drawn into capitalism at its most repugnant, and the two early slaving expeditions in which Drake participated, these are not to be dismissed and I don't dismiss them. But are our indignant twenty-somethings in a position, four centuries on, to hand down judgement quite so magisterially? You like that sporty look, do you? Very nice, I agree. Where were those tennis shoes stitched together, in return for what wage exactly? And whoever made them, do you think she was white?

The Cold War version of Drake which a few of us were still growing up on in the Seventies feels dubious by now, granted. It's unsurprising that we take our revenge either by cutting him out altogether or by re-inventing him as *the* pioneer of our piratical 'globalisation'. And pretty pictures in his notebook notwithstanding, he was, arguably, one of its pioneers. But I have tried here to suggest that there was more to his achievement, and more to his context, than can sensibly be reduced to his least admirable actions as a privateer.

four

We were caught in a Force Nine gale once on our way back from the Scillies – entertaining a stoical self-image at the time I stayed up on deck and storm-watched all the way back to Penzance. A crossing which normally takes two and a half hours took eight but I wedged myself as tight as I could into a corner which shielded me from the worst of it. Big as our ship and bigger, waves towered and teetered or one of them shattered on impact and went hissing and slithering across our decks. The RMV Scillonian III needs a relatively shallow draft for the waters around the islands, which can make rough crossings very rough indeed. Through half-closed eyes I found I could just about imagine this the Year of Our Lord Fifteen Hundred and Seventy-Eight and this our proud galleon battling a hurricano through the Straits of Magellan. It helped to pass the time anyway. We seemed not so much to be advancing towards our destination as foiling violent and repeated attempts to make the boat go backwards. From the security of my improvised look-out the line of the deck reared right up then dropped as alarmingly far below the horizon as it had only just been tossed above it.

In between waves came the reassuring tremor of engines still working. At the foot of a cliff, as the coastline crawled by, lay the up-turned hull of the *Union Star*. I'd sung carols a couple of Christmases ago for the families of its crew and the families of those who died on the lifeboat that went to its rescue. I'd fallen into a kind of trance, I suppose, staring into each wall of water as it approached, the ship rolling and recoiling from the last or lurching into the next. And here came one now that looked much like the others, until a dolphin leapt out of it. That woke me up alright but it was one dolphin for one leap only then gone again, back into that seething mass of verticals and horizontals, planes not so much intersecting as randomly colliding and buckling as they did so. But somewhere inside it all now was that mysterious dolphin. And I had a story to explain what I'd stuck to this strange vigil for.

Waiting for my first interview and needing to keep an eye on the time I have breakfast with my alarm clock at a table on the Esplanade. Twenty-five years have elapsed and I have made appointments with people by email. I am in Plymouth, with dictaphone and plenty of tapes, with a bag on my shoulder and PhDs to meet. It's a tricky one, as we've seen, asking the sea to mean something, because that in turn means asking what kinds of knowledge, what registers of expression matter more – which will mean asking why.

There's a young couple on the beach below trying to skim pebbles and the water is smooth and green and glittering in the morning light. The pebbles are the wrong shape though – they can never get more than three or four skips out of them. Dog-walkers at another table discuss the dolphins that were in yesterday and two guys talk car-parts over a cooked breakfast. There are several large warships in the Sound with others out at sea but I've been sitting here some time before I notice there's a submarine too, moored over by the breakwater. There is a cheese on toast that someone has ordered but no one is here to eat. The warships move solemnly about, on some kind of joint exercise. The couple is giving up on those pebbles. They just lob one every now and again.

What the sea means.

That earliest contact with the day stays with me through a morning of filling in forms at reception desks and clipping on visitor's badges. I have one interview at the Plymouth Marine

Laboratory, another at the Marine Biological Association. In the lobby of either building I am met by persons not wearing badges, then conducted along corridors by the same, persons travelling at speed as they escort you, at home here, persons who have seen all these interesting photographs on the wall hundreds of times.

The man I meet at the Plymouth Marine Laboratory is compiling a report on how the Marine Protected Area in Lyme Bay has effected the local economy. He is from Kenya and worked for years on marine reserves in the Indian Ocean and the Mediterranean, while his PhD in environmental science is from here. Oh yes, he smiles, in some ways fishermen are much the same way everywhere, or everywhere he's been. And so are the conservationists.

The marine reserves in Kenya were set up without consultation, imposed from above. Doing it that way worked no better than the endless 'voluntary agreements' with fishermen who went on dredging the Lyme Bay reefs here regardless until the government banned it. 'The exact formula is different everywhere, but everywhere you have to engage with those directly affected, listen to what they're telling you, and you have to establish credible sanctions against infringements. You have to do both.'

If we ask the sea to mean something now, perhaps it means as much as anything the people who live around it - how similar we are everywhere in our fascination with it and our arguments over it. That I'm even having this conversation, that knowledge about how to organise these reserves now travels freely and continuously, via people like this, from the Lyme Bay reefs, to the northern shores of the Med to the East African coast – isn't that what it *means* now?

At the Marine Biological Association (MBA), a short walk along the Hoe, the researcher I meet has an exhibition about plankton on at London Zoo, the BBC has put some of his photographs on their website and there's a book coming out. That is getting pretty famous by planktologist standards. The MBA, the oldest such association in the world, is housed in a building directly adjacent to the Citadel – the Naval Headquaters – marines are lounging on the ramparts next door. The two buildings share a magnificent view over the Sound but the MBA emerged from a very different set of sea-meanings, as my interviewee is happy to explain.

‘Darwin assumed that life must have originated by some spontaneous generation in the sea. This had already been the general assumption for several generations – his grandfather Erasmus had thought the same. If life, the argument ran, had somehow started with tiny marine organisms, relatively simple in structure, then where better to look for the clues to life’s origin than among unicellular marine invertebrates?’

As a student in Edinburgh, Darwin filled notebooks with observations from his walks along the Firth of Forth. He was looking for sea-sponges, because these had been identified from the fossil record as a very ancient – possibly the most ancient - form of life. But the zoologists of the day knew little more about them than Aristotle had been able to find out more than two thousand years earlier, not even whether they were plants or animals. Aristotle had thought they were animals but how did they reproduce, in that case? What purposes did their bizarre structure serve? Alongside the sponges in those notebooks are detailed descriptions of cuttlefish and sea mice and star fish. There were dredging expeditions, too, on the local oysterboats. Such were the circumstances in which the greatest scientist of his age began to ask questions about the origins of life.

'Everyone credits Darwin's finches and the Galapagos – which were the seed-corn in a way for his theory – but it was well before that, with marine biology, that he really made his start as a scientist. And when he got back from the Galapagos – what does he spend the next eight years doing? Putting the taxonomy and phylogeny of barnacles in order. *Barnacles!* That's how he builds his reputation as a scientist: again, with marine biology. And all the while that idea he had on the *Beagle* is still there – he's peering down microscopes not just describing but asking himself all the time *how* these differences came about? As responses to what?

'So the study of marine organisms was at the heart of his inquiry into the origin of species and into the origins of life itself. Not just for Darwin – it was true for scientists from around the world – there were dozens of them sending him specimens and corresponding. Marine biology has always been a very collaborative affair. It's international by its nature. So this Marine Biological Association here in Plymouth, and the others that were set up around the same time - one in Naples and another at Woods Hole in

Massachusetts - they were all part of this same wider inquiry.'

The MBA is home to one of the longest-running research-programs anywhere into the world's oceans. Scientists look to marine invertebrates now less for insight into the origins of life than for indications as to its long-range prospects. The Continuous Plankton Recorder Survey had already been running since 1931, decades before the question of global warming ever arose. That is just what makes it so important now. Sensitive to the minutest changes in their surroundings, plankton make up the best indicators we have as to changes in that environment. As an earlier age might have put it, the Survey's insights into the life of the oceans have a value 'far passing all riches and earthly treasure'.

The 'recorders' themselves are kept in a workshop downstairs. There are usually twenty or so of these devices 'out' at any time. Ranged on wooden shelves are those currently 'in'. Squat, painted silver, each has a small armature at the front ending in a ring. Manufactured in Plymouth to a design which has hardly changed in eighty years, they are deployed mainly in the North Sea, North Atlantic and North Pacific. That ring is for the rope by which they are attached to the freighters and ferries which tow them about at a depth of six metres. Any vessel which follows the same route regularly and at a steady speed is ideal and over many years relationships have been built with the shipping companies which participate.

Each recorder is about the size of a television camera only with a snub metal nose where the lens would be. Instead of a film inside there is a roll of silk gauze which is slowly wound from one spool to another. One roll of silk 'records' 450 miles of ocean – as the recorder is towed a stream of sea-water passes through this gauze, which traps any plankton and preserves them in formalin. These rolls of 'film' are then 'developed' under microscopes back in Plymouth, in the laboratory next to where the recorders are kept.

Where any given creature has come from can easily be read off from charts hung on the otherwise bare walls in there. These display the shipping lanes used by the contributing vessels, radiating out across the world's oceans in blunt pencil. Under one of the microscopes as I am shown around there is a 'copepod' – a kind of plankton. It was collected by a freighter off the coast of Nova Scotia. It is from a species usually found in tropical or sub-tropical waters but often occurring off the Canadian coast, carried there by the Gulf Stream.

If we were looking now to adjust the global system which we have built, make it more accountable to the longer-term interests of life on this planet, we would not, most of us, search for the answers where Dee did. Conversations with angels and the conversion of the savages are by now problematic in several important respects. Alchemy and astrology likewise. But does it follow that our global system must therefore, as at present, attune itself to no long-term reality at all?

What if Dee's most valuable contribution was in his tireless efforts to link up a divided Europe, just as it was sheering so dangerously apart? At the perilous moment of its creation, he tried to breathe some supranational, collaborative sense into this quarrelsome and aggressive new civilisation. As the scientific revolution gets underway, he both actively promotes it and also begins his own parallel search: for forms of self-knowledge that can keep pace with these advances in our understanding of, and power over, the world around us. He may have articulated this latter search in languages which are now mostly lost to us, but that surely does not invalidate the search itself. In fact we are more than ever now in need of answers to the kind of questions he was already then asking.

Plankton Surveys were certainly not the kind of magic Dee had in mind, but they have a certain pedigree all the same. Darwin sailed from Plymouth in December 1831 and the following entry is found in one of his *Beagle* notebooks, two years into the five-year voyage: 'During our different passages south of the Plata I often towed astern a net made of bunting and thus caught many curious animals.' The same notebooks testify to his close study of what he discovered in this way. Darwin too collaborated with fellow-scientists the world over as he pondered his own world-changing theory. He would surely have seen a global survey like this run for more than eighty years as the marvel which it is.

If we were looking for a collaborative purpose like Dee's or Darwin's working in the present, might it not be precisely to something like the Continuous Plankton Recorder that we should turn? The northward advance of warm water plankton species over the past thirty years has proceeded at approximately 23 km per year on average, with noticeable acceleration since 1995. This change is real, it is measurable (see figure 5), and its impact on marine ecosystems (just as over-fishing was already doing its worse) is already being felt. A recent study showed that British fishing vessels in 1937 landed fourteen times as much fish by weight as their modern counterparts.[12] So how do we translate such data into the way we live? Can we temper our effect on the natural world, match all this 'data' with a corresponding self-knowledge? Or not?

I handed in that second visitor's badge and walked out into the midday sunshine on the Hoe. The warships were fewer and much further out now, and the submarine had gone. Here was the lunch-time crowd come to enjoy the view. I joined it and the Roscoff ferry leaving harbour seemed to participate in the festive mood.

The ship's whistle on that ferry may not have a very *Golden Hind*-ish or *Beagle*an ring to it but I knew now that every time that boat pulls out of Plymouth Sound it is towing a plankton recorder. In so doing it is like other ships sailing out of other ports the world over, ships you would never have suspected of having any 'other' purpose beyond moving people and goods about.

I took a day or two to look around. Plymouth, Point of Famous Departures, the one I used to know all about, is present mainly in the form of gateways. On the massive stone gateway to an old barracks for the marines, the weather-vane points south-west, rusted solid on its mounting. Fanfares of purple buddleia sprout from between the blocks of its pediment. It stands very monumentally at the edge of a housing estate which now covers the site. The gateway to a vanished ordnance factory leads to a little outlet which sells fishing gear 'and much much more'. They're everywhere and the information boards which draw your attention to some of them invariably describe them as 'imposing', but is 'imposing' the word?

The Mayflower Memorial on Sutton Quay is in the form of a stone arch: it opens onto the destiny of the English-speaking peoples and an elaborate little balcony paid for by American Friends. The archway built into a wall behind the aquarium serves to conceal from view a multi-storey car park. What do all these gateways open onto now? The wide world – Sierra Leone, Tahiti - or the multi-storey, with its concrete pillars and inclined ramp coiled round a central grey light-well?

The Victorians still knew which it was: the Hoe is their confident gesture towards everything out there. Its flagpoles and statues are the long row of medals which their England awarded itself for conspicuous gallantry. Newfoundland, Nova Albion, New Zealand, New South Wales – did so much newness ever disappear over any horizon as disappeared over this one? Even our grandparents could still screw a brass plaque to that wall: Charlie Chaplin passed this way to board a liner in 1931.

Wandering past St Andrews I stopped inside and had that discussion with a church warden which was the starting-point for these reflections. Dee and the others dreamt of some way over the roof of the world to Cathay, of a commodity to be found there 'far passing all riches and earthly treasure'. The most obvious outcome was Drake unleashed on Spanish and Portuguese shipping in the Pacific. Elizabeth was able to pay off the whole of her foreign debt with her share of the proceeds and to found the Levant Company with some of what was left over. From the profits of the Levant Company the East India Company was eventually formed.[13] And so on. Attempting

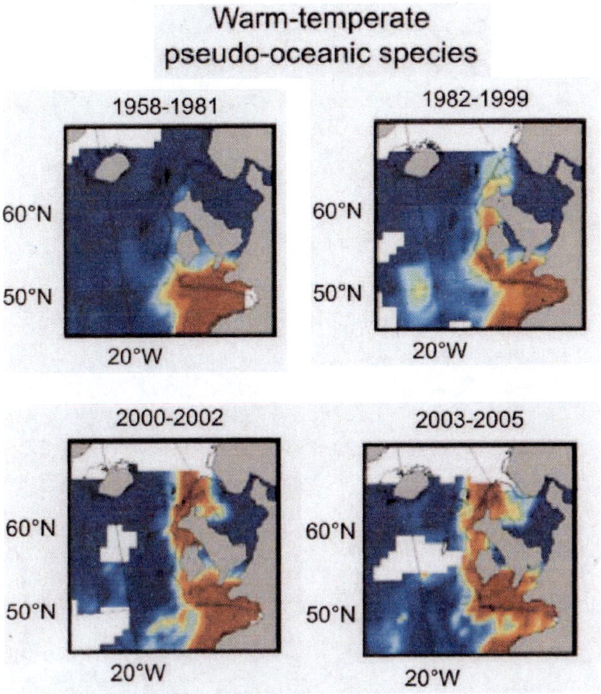

Figure 5: Northward advance of warm-temperate plankton species over four decades, using data collected by the Continuous Plankton Survey[14]

Figure 6 Grey phalaropes. Photo by Tom Brereton

to relegate all of that to something secondary is futile. But returning to Plymouth there must have been, even for Drake, some sense of another dimension to what he had achieved than the gold he was using for ballast.

The welcome he came home to, not to mention some of the graffiti it inspired, was drawing on deeper, stranger sources, surely, than the sort of fuss which attends any lottery win, even one as colossal as this. Plymouth Sound and Francis Drake might become for England very roughly what Cape Canaveral and Neil Armstrong are to the United States, Drake might be revered for centuries as the epitome of national and personal self-aggrandisement, but does any of that prove Dee was wrong or deluded to have hoped for something finer from the new science?

five

It's one thing of course to imagine you'd love to live in the beautiful West Country, where you grew up etc etc. Do it and there are times when it feels like the worst mistake you ever made. On an evening like the one I'm describing all those other places in the world where you would be so much happier rise up and mock you in the form of dusk in a small town. What *was* so wrong with that Vancouver idea, after all? The answer, on such an evening as this, is Emphatically Nothing. Getting sentimental won't help. Any small town can feel like a sentence and love mine as I by and large do, it is no exception.

For evenings like these there is the pub, for which my pretext shall be a book I want to get out and read somewhere – it's about the *Odyssey*, in fact – a book I don't tire of and am glad to be writing about. Which is how come I am some way into my pint before I realise that I am observed.

I first met Tom in the queue for the Portsmouth–Santander ferry. He is drinking at a table nearby now but he was clasping a telescope and tripod then, and standing in a group of others doing the same. Having stood in similar groups myself, I went over and asked what they were hoping to see. He had arranged with the ferry-line to run a survey of whales and dolphins from the decks of their ships. He spoke with a Manchester accent so I was all the more startled to discover that he had in fact only just moved to the same small town near Lyme Bay in which I, too, was a recent arrival.

He is, I have learnt since, an encyclopaedically knowledgeable naturalist, and good at organisations too. He set up 'Marinelife' a few years later and by making observations from local fishing-boats has built up an intimate understanding of the area's off-shore wildlife, mainly its birds and cetaceans, or 'megafauna'. It's a quiet pub, so we are able to exchange thoughts on the *Odyssey* and the latest Marinelife news without difficulty. His news is good: EU funding to charter his own boat for survey work in Lyme Bay and the Western Approaches to the Channel. Might I be interested in helping out?

So much for Vancouver. *Might* I?! Going out for a drink and a sulk isn't always the wrong answer. Whatever else my home town might be, it is also the kind of place where you run into people who casually offer you things like this. The weather looked set fine when he called to confirm. The catamaran would leave Dartmouth at 8 am.

We drove through the dark most of the way and still only made it with twenty minutes to spare. A 5 AM start, a 7-30 arrival, thermos flasks and the sea. The catamaran was just filling up at the fuel barge in the middle of the harbour but between there and the landing-stage it developed a problem. Our pilot had no sooner brought the boat alongside than he disappeared into his cabin to re-emerge in diving-suit and goggles. The propeller, it turned out, had snagged on a plastic bag so he surfaced asking for a knife. Not to lose any more time he started the engine as soon as he was back on board and gave me the wheel to steer us out of the harbour while he dried himself and changed back into his clothes.

According to the port book, a ship called the *Laurel* sailed out of Dartmouth in 1618. Drake and Hawkins, the Armada and the search for El Dorado were already history. The first two were long dead, the Armada was a fading memory and Raleigh was in the Tower with only months to live. King James had cracked down on the privateers in return for a deal with Spain allowing English boats to trade freely in South American ports. The *Paul of Plimmouth* had been the first

English boat to trade with Brazil via West Africa, returning almost a century earlier with tropical hard wood and '1 dozen elephant's teeth weighing 1 cwt'. Now the trade revived. The *Laurel* took a cargo of 'knives, beads, spades and thimbles.' There was nothing remarkable about her journey. Indeed it's this atmosphere of business-as-usual which is perhaps the most striking thing now about those port books.

The *Laurel* returned after eight months with 'a cargo of timber.' It seems the European powers had agreed, for now, to patch up their religious differences and join in a combined assault on a new enemy: tropical rainforest. Their campaign has, notoriously, continued. But was it a diversion from old religious conflicts, or did it, rather, mark the start, in some way scarcely noticed at the time, of a new kind of 'religious difference'? Those for whom the world is now there for the plundering, because we can, and those for whom it is certainly there, but not for that.

Our crew that morning as we left the harbour was a retired Methodist minister and a cameraman made redundant by cuts at the BBC. There was an estate agent from Cornwall laid off in the recession, doing odd jobs for the Council now. He'd seen the snowy owl when it appeared in the Hayle Estuary and the Gyr falcon too. He'd spend all his time on survey boats if he didn't have to work, he said. And there were the two formally trained biologists. Our pilot took over the wheel again. It was thirty miles to the transect, where the actual surveying would begin.

There's an in-built democracy about bird-watchers which often makes of such gatherings a sort of low-key social experiment. None of us naturally very gregarious, we stood bunched at the front of the boat, introducing ourselves after the peculiarly absent fashion of our sub-culture, each one clutching his or her binoculars like a first drink. On a convenient ledge data-sheets had been left, fastened to clipboards: from each other we turned to the open water around us as we ventured out upon it. Conversation narrowed, for now, to bird-names and what o'clock.

One of the rarest birds in Europe is being seen more and more often off the South West of England. The Balearic shearwater is shifting its feeding-grounds northwards from its former strongholds in the Mediterranean and Biscay. Its rarity and the recent shift in its behaviour are between them what recommended Tom's work to the EU – a bird I've never seen was effectively paying for this survey-work.

I still haven't seen one and the sky remained of a uniform grey from dawn to dusk. It was one of those charmed days nonetheless. We were about half-way to the transect when thirty or forty dolphins came alongside. We downed data-sheets and shed our self-consciousness: wherever you looked over the side there were five or six of them and in their effortless way they made us feel part of a fortunate enterprise. They gave us their blessing. Through green water we studied the stripes of blue, yellow and grey for however many minutes it was, before all as suddenly as they had appeared they vanished in search of fresh entertainment. In the shelter behind the pilot's cabin we hurriedly returned cameras to cases and got back to neglected datasheets, knowing our luck had set fair and knitted together in that knowledge as we hadn't been before.

We reached the transect a couple of hours later and changed course to follow it. A more serious kind of data-sheet appeared, with more boxes for more detail and there would be plenty of detail to fill them with. The transect took us and our 40-footer right out into the shipping lanes, among Panama-registered freighters and towering ferries and quickly passing warships.

Our pilot coped with their bow-waves as best he could but it was an uneasy ride at times. There are several things you notice about the middle of the Channel from a little survey boat. From a modern ferry the sheer size of what you're on tends to make most of the other ships around you seem 'normal size'. All those shops and cafés and the speed of the crossing distract you from even asking. A couple of meadow pipits went by, skipping specks miles from the nearest meadow, crossing over from France a few feet above the water.

The containers stacked high on the decks of a freighter were badges of trade and industry. The guns and the grey of battleships went as arrogantly as ever about their sovereignty and security business, with or without Russian submarines to chase. An occasional yacht signalled leisure and style, or stocks and shares at least. A Dutch pelagic trawler dragged a vast net eastwards up the Channel after shoals of sprats – each of these was engaged in its full-scale and accredited occupation. 'If binoculars and knowledge and data-sheets are all you have to show for yourselves, maybe being tossed about on our bow-waves is just what you need - most of you look as if you could do with a good shaking up,' said the traffic in this very busy and important shipping-lane.

We re-crossed it and continued the transect westwards, then headed back towards Dartmouth through calmer inshore waters. There were more birds and dolphins and porpoises but it's a conversation, rather, which has stayed with me from the end of our trip. Tom was looking out specially sharp for birds of the Canadian Arctic – they are not infrequently visitors off Devon and Cornwall at certain times of the year. Sabine's and ring-billed gulls and grey phalaropes (figure 6). Autumn gales usually carry a few North American butterflies across with them.

We were passing places along the Devon coast that I recognised even a mile or so off-shore from HW's long-ago bird-watching trips, Slapton Sands, Salcombe, places I haven't been back to since. But Tom's talk of migrants from the Canadian Arctic prompted a new kind of reflection now. That these monarch butterflies and grey phalaropes must have been regularly 'discovering' the Old World long millennia before the first European humans credited themselves with having 'discovered' the New one. It doesn't, of course, detract from the achievement of those explorers, because human beings cannot be reproached for not having wings, but for a moment the thought of it conjured up a biosphere ceaselessly on the move and our own restlessness, right down to our dawn-starts for Dartmouth or bad-day Vancouver-moments, as a part of that.

The will to knowledge, from a romantic walk along the beach to sailing round the world, from that bird flying by to the process by which even the theory of evolution, it turns out, was arrived at with the sea's help. The memory and history and science all encoded in this coastline and this evening, each speaking through forms of knowledge which discovered me quite as much as I ever discovered them and which made me who I am.

On the home-run now, data-sheets crammed with a rich harvest of biro-jottings, we'd been lucky all the way out and had remained so all the way back in. The cloud cover never really broke but it thinned as the sun sank, suffusing us and everything around us with a pale orange glow. Then darkness began to fall. Dartmouth, by the time we reached it, was a steep-sided creek with shadowy hills piled above. Its slopes were hung with rows of house-lights and street-lights one above the other. Like some fantastical underground community in cross-section, it was so little like anywhere I'd seen before that we could almost have been arriving for the first time in a completely unknown country.

Suggested Reading:

Sir Francis Drake: The Construction of a Hero, Bruce Wathen, D.S.Brewer, 2009: I would like to express a special debt to Mr Wathen. His remarkable book deserves wider recognition.

The Queen's Corsair, Alexander McKee, Souvenir Press, 1978
John Dee's Natural Philosophy, Nicholas Clulee, Routledge, 1988
John Dee: The World of an Elizabethan Magus, Peter French, Routledge, 1972
Tudor Geography 1485-1583, Eva Taylor, Methuen, 1930
Darwin and the Barnacle, Rebecca Stott, Faber and Faber, 2003
The Open Sea, Vol. 1, Alister Hardy (invented the Plankton Recorder), Collins, 1956

Special thanks to:

The Dorset and Devon Wildlife Trusts
The Bridport Environment Group
Stephen Mangi of the Plymouth Marine Lab,
Richard Kirby of the Marine Biological Association, Plymouth
Tom Brereton of Marinelife
(Volunteers for Marinelife surveys should contact Kate at kate.lewis@marine_life.org.uk)

Endnotes:

[1] David Waters, *The Art of Navigation in Elizabethan and early Stuart England,* Greenwich, 1958
[2] Mary W. Helms, *Ulysses' Sail,* Princeton, 1988
[3] George Best, *A True Discourse of the late Voyages of Discoverie for the finding of a passage to Cathaya*, 1578
[4] From Dee's marginal annotations to his copy of *Historie Del S.D.Fernando Colombo* (a biography of Christopher Columbus written by his son) Venice, 1571.
[5] William H. Sherman, *John Dee,* p.181, Amherst, 1995
[6] See Nicholas Clulee, *John Dee's Natural History Re-Visited*, in *John Dee: Interdisciplinary Studies in English Renaissance Thought*, Springer, 2007
[7] S.T.Coleridge, *The Constitution of the Church and State*, 1830
[8] Mary Midgley, *The Use and Uselessness of Learning*, in *Utopias, Dolphins and Computers,* Routledge, 1996
[9] Walter Benjamin, *One Way Street*, in *Reflections*, Schocken Books, 2007
[10] *Boethian Number Theory,* a translation of *De Institutione Arithmetrica*, Amsterdam, 1983
[11] In Plutarch's *Quaestiones Platonicae*
[12]Callum Roberts et al. *The Effects of Industrial Fishing on UK Fisheries*, Nature Communications, May 2010
[13] J.M.Keynes *A Treatise on Money*, London, 1930
[14] Grégory Beaugrand, 'Rapid Biogeographical plankton shift in the North Atlantic Ocean' in *Global Change Biology*, Blackwell, 2009. Reproduced with permission.